Put yourself in the polaroid!

*"I made a Ryan Gosling colouring book, because I assumed
that everyone would want to colour him in"*

love
mel
x

Colour Me Good Ryan Gosling
Designed & Illustrated by Mel Simone Elliott

Published by
I LOVE MEL
United Kingdom
978-0-9567208
June 2012

I Love Mel is a trading name of Brolly Associates Ltd
www.ilovemel.me mel@ilovemel.me
©M S Elliott 2012

ISBN Number
978-0-9573148-3-2

Distributed in the United States and Canada by SCB Distributors.
Distributed outside of the United States and Canada by Turnaround Publisher Services.